Original title:
The Tropics in My Room

Copyright © 2025 Creative Arts Management OÜ
All rights reserved.

Author: William Hawthorne
ISBN HARDBACK: 978-1-80581-824-3
ISBN PAPERBACK: 978-1-80581-351-4
ISBN EBOOK: 978-1-80581-824-3

Journey to an Inner Shore

In my corner, a palm tree sways,
With a beach ball lost in my gaze.
A flamingo lounges, sips iced tea,
Dreaming of vacation—oh, to be free!

Cacti wear shades, looking quite cool,
As I navigate this plastic pool.
An ocean breeze, but no waves in sight,
Just me and my snacks, a tropical night.

The sun is bright, but it's just my lamp,
A towel draped over my pet hamster, Champ.
He's the captain, steering my ship of dreams,
Through the vast lands of couch cushions and creams.

Whimsical journeys, well, I'm quite grand,
With seashells scattered, I make my stand.
Each wave a laugh, each tide a cheer,
In this little paradise, I conquor fear!

Exotic Echoes in Quiet Corners

In a plant pot lives a parrot,
Squawking tales of near and far.
My cat's the finest pirate here,
Yet fears the jungle—a house plant star.

Coconut scents in the air drift,
An adventure brewed just a sip.
Socks on my feet, they dance and twirl,
As I navigate this indoor whirl.

Ferns and Fantasies

Ferns are wizards in disguise,
Casting spells of leafy cheer.
They whisper secrets in their green,
While I pretend I have no fear.

A hibiscus hat upon my head,
I strut around like a proud fool.
In my kingdom of pots and dirt,
It's the silliest of rules—no tool!

Hummingbird Hues

Hummingbirds zip past my ear,
With hues that spark the day anew.
They mock my dance, so unrefined,
Yet fly in circles, graceful too.

Caught in a mishap with my snack,
A slice of mango, a bold bite—
Swiped from the table, it took wing,
"Oh, what a mess!" I laugh in plight.

The Lushness of Imagined Shores

From pillows piled, a beach appears,
With fluffy waves and laughter bright.
The sand is all just crumbs, I cheer,
And sunbathing's strong in bed tonight.

Seashells play the tune of bliss,
While crickets serenade the view.
I sip my drink, a chocolate bliss,
And laugh at dreams that feel so true.

Sunlit Fantasies in the Afternoon

A sunbeam sneaks in, oh what a sight,
My cat becomes a lion in pure delight.
The ice cream melts, but who can complain?
I sip from my glass as if it were champagne.

Tropical prints dance on my wall,
I swear that they giggle, they're having a ball.
The ceiling fan spins tales of its own,
Whisking away worries that might be grown.

When Coconuts Grow Near My Heart

Coconuts giggle from high on a tree,
They'd make perfect hats, don't you agree?
With daisies in hand, I throw them a wink,
They just roll their eyes as if they can think.

I named my pet fern Sir Bubbles McLeaf,
He's a splendid companion, beyond all belief.
His fronds sway to music only he hears,
While I trade my worries for palm tree cheers.

Petite Orchid Serenades

Little orchids glance, aren't they sweet?
They whisper their secrets, oh what a treat!
I dance with the shadows, they join in my fun,
As petals twirl softly beneath the bright sun.

In pots filled with laughter, they sing out so clear,
Telling me jokes that only I hear.
The sunbathes us all in a warm, silly glow,
While I wonder how far these giggles can go.

Palm-Tree Daydreams

Palm trees debate if they're tall or they're wise,
While I lounge below, enjoying the skies.
They sway to the rhythm of breezes so light,
Inviting me deeper into this delight.

Daydreams take flight on their majestic leaves,
They tell wild tales no one believes.
With laughter like waves, crashing all around,
In this paradise, joy knows no bounds.

A Hideaway of Hibiscus

In a corner green, I weave my chair,\nWith floral prints that dance, they dare.\nAbove my head, a parrot sips,\nWhile my cat plots onsite, just in case of slips.

Pineapple plants with googly eyes,\nGossiping secrets, oh how time flies.\nThe kumquat laughs as I take a seat,\nWhile a coconut laughs at my clumsy feet.

I wear a crown of folds and leaves,\nWith a smile that's hard to believe.\nOrchids tease me, bloom and pout,\nWhile I spill my lemonade about.

In this room, I rule like a queen,\nWhere plants plot, and nothing's routine.\nWith every bloom, a giggle's chime,\nIt's a hideaway where the silliness climbs.

Melodies of the Monsoon

Raindrops tap dance on my shoe,\nSinging songs of mischief too.\nGreen umbrellas flying high,\nA snail's race, oh my, oh my!

In a puddle, I take a leap,\nWatch out, my socks, do not weep!\nThe mango tree shakes, it knows the tune,\nWhile two frogs croak a silly croon.

I sip tea from a coconut mug,\nWhile thunder joins with a playful shrug.\nThe rain has turned the world to glee,\nIn this wild concert, nothing's free.

As droplets spin around my head,\nI laugh at all, no sense of dread.\nA giggle here, a splish, a splash,\nIn my quirkiest rain dance bash!

Dappled Sunshine in Creased Pages

Sunlight streams from crooked blinds,\nIlluminating tales of naughty minds.\nMy books conspire with dust bunnies,\nWhispering plans over giggly honeys.

Each page flips with a gentle sigh,\nWhile sunbeams wink and butterflies fly.\nThe cat's a judge, with a sleepy stare,\nAs my stories dance in the sun-drenched air.

Plot twists hidden in flower pots,\nAdventures brewed in coffee spots.\nWhile I stitch my dreams with a playful nail,\nWhere fiction meets reality, it's all fairytale.

My quilt, a treasure, bright and bold,\nStores secrets of mischief yet untold.\nIn this cozy nook where laughter blooms,\nDappled sunshine welcomes the happy tunes.

The Lullaby of Lush Greens

Underneath the leafy chimes,\nA giggling garden bell doth rhyme.\nWith ferns that sway, and vines that tease,\nIt's a jungle gym for my germs of glee.

A hammock swings with echoes bright,\nWhile shy orchids blush in flight.\nThe sunflowers turn, and so do I,\nTrading seeds in a merry high.

Lizards prance with silly tails,\nPlotting stories of tiny trails.\nIn my little jungle, adventure's near,\nWith each flutter, a chuckle here.

Coconut shells, my treasure chest,\nFilled with giggles, I must confess.\nAs the lullaby echoes sweet and clear,\nIn this green haven, I hold dear.

Basking in Indoor Sunlight

In a world of soft warmth and light,
I'm sipping juice, what a delight!
The cat claims my sunbeam throne,
While I question my houseplant's tone.

A lizard slides by, totally nonchalant,
In my tropical faux-pas, I can't help but flaunt.
With sunglasses on, I take a sip,
Pretending I'm on a vacation trip.

Where the Frangipani Blooms

A lone flower sits on my desk,
It's fragrant and slightly grotesque.
Do they care if I droop or wilt?
Such elegance with no guilt!

My neighbor's cat strolls by with flair,
Thinking my paradise is his lair.
He knocks down my pot, oh what a shame,
Wearing my peace like it's a game!

Ocean Breeze Beneath My Roof

I've got a fan that shakes the air,
Making my hair dance with flair.
Each gust whispers secrets, oh so rare,
Like my laundry hanging with little care.

Pineapple pizza is a big debate,
In my tropical kingdom, it's a first-rate plate.
But when the breeze gets a bit too bold,
It sends my snacks flying, uncontrolled!

A Canopy of Colorful Thoughts

Painted walls in hues so bright,
They clash but give me sheer delight.
Each corner hides a memory, fun,
A garden party with my pet dog, run!

I often ponder where to go,
With my trusty snack, I'm good to flow.
As I plot my comical escape,
I realize I'm already trapped in tape!

A Room Filled with Warmth

In a corner, a parrot squawks loud,
A goldfish swims, it's quite a crowd.
Cactus dances, sways in delight,
As the disco ball spins, oh what a sight!

My socks are lost, where did they flee?
Perhaps the monkey took them, you see?
Bananas peel themselves with a grin,
This living room jungle, let the fun begin!

Rainforest Vibrations

The ceiling fan spins, whizzing along,
As insects do the cha-cha, singing their song.
A sloth hangs out, sipping on brunch,
While the sofa has thrown itself a wild punch!

Lianas swing low, right by the TV,
I plug in my phone, oh woe is me!
The Wi-Fi is weak, a jaguar's hidden,
But laughter echoes loud, there's no one forbidden!

The Color of Dreams and Sun

Pillow forts built for a tropical bash,
With bright shades of pink, oh what a clash!
Llamas join in for some pillow fights,
Under twinkling lights that scale heights!

Tropical smoothies spill on the floor,
As pineapple prints dance out the door.
The coffee table is now a treasure chest,
Full of odd socks, munchies, and jest!

Sun-dappled Corners of Elegance

Curtains flutter like a flamingo's dance,
Every corner begs for a wild romance.
The fridge hums softly, a serenade sweet,
While a toucan munches on some rare treat.

Hammocks swing with a giggling sound,
As the dust bunnies tumble, oh, what a round!
A pineapple hat rests on my head,
In this stylish chaos, I snooze instead!

Vibrant Blooms in a Quiet Space

Petunias speckled with bright cheer,
Whispering secrets only they hear.
A cactus dressed in a party hat,
Wonders why no one gives him a pat.

Sunlight dances on painted leaves,
While a mischievous vine deceives.
A fern plays peek-a-boo with the light,
Claiming it's the star of the night!

Mornings Sipping Tropical Air

Mango-scented dreams at dawn,
Wake me up, let's laugh and yawn.
Pineapple juice in sippy cups,
Tickling our noses as it spills up.

Birds sing tunes of silly song,
While a lizard struts all day long.
Sip that sunshine, taste the breeze,
Finding fun in swaying trees!

A Dance of Petals and Light

A sunflower tops the fashion game,
Twisting and spinning, seeking fame.
Lilies giggle in shades of white,
While daisies join the up-all-night.

Bright hibiscus wear polka dots,
While orchids cry "We love your spots!"
Petal parties under the sun,
Every bloom agrees that it's fun!

Tropical Essence in Stillness

In a corner, a palm leans near,
Pretending to listen, feeling sheer.
Green Coca-Cola in a glass cup,
Who knew a leaf could shake it up?

A sleepy cactus yawns with glee,
"Not my fault, it's too hot for me!"
Laughter ripples through the air,
In this wild and leafy affair.

Ferns and Shadows

Ferns whisper secrets of the night,
Casting shadows, oh what a sight!
A monkey's laugh, a coconut's swing,
In my cozy nook, I'm the jungle king.

Potted plants play hide and seek,
Mischief grows in every peak.
Lizards dance on the window ledge,
With a cheeky leap, they make a pledge.

An umbrella drinks my cappuccino,
Pretending it's a stylish casino.
A fake parrot caws with flair,
Who knew fun could fill the air?

Bamboo straws sipping sunlight bright,
In a room where it's always light.
What a party, no need to roam,
Life's a joke in my leafy home.

Invisible Canopy

Beneath a sky that's not quite there,
I wear my best sunhat with flare.
Invisible rays paint my walls,
While a chattering squirrel calls.

My ceiling's an endless blue,
Where dreams of palm trees come into view.
Invisible leaves fall with glee,
Oh, how mischievous they can be!

A flip-flop lost in a chair,
Thinks it's still on the sandy fare.
Little critters in my dreams,
Have wild parties, or so it seems!

An oasis of laughter, a giggle-filled room,
Where every corner can burst with bloom.
So, cheers to this world, quite unplanned,
With humor in every grain of sand!

Petals Under My Pillow

Petals tucked where dreams reside,
I wake up laughing, oh what a ride!
A butterfly danced upon my hair,
Kissed my cheek with a floral air.

Sneaky beetles play on my desk,
Like little jesters, they're quite grotesque.
One tried to steal a sip of tea,
While I giggled and let it be.

The sun peeks in, with a grin on its face,
Turning my room into a sunshine race.
Piles of petals, my cheerful spree,
Sometimes, a bloom ends up in my knee!

Oh, sleep escapes in this floral blend,
With dreams of laughter as my best friend.
A soft, sweet slumber, but who's to say,
That morning won't copy my playful display?

Echoes of a Distant Shore

Echoes drift from a far-off sea,
As I dance with joy, just me and me.
A wave crashes down upon my bed,
Oh, the fish tell tales in my head!

Seashells giggle on the floor,
Telling secrets, who could ask for more?
I join their chatter, a playful crowd,
In this sea of dreams, I'm feeling proud!

An ocean breeze whips through the room,
As my socks become surfboards to zoom.
Laughing crabs now gather round,
Tickled by tides of mirth profound!

Each wave mocks the sand that's near,
Whispers of laughter fill the sphere.
With every echo, I am free,
In this joyful haven, just me and me!

Vibrant Canopy of Thought

Under leaves of silly dreams,
Laughter echoes, or so it seems.
Sunlight dances with a grin,
Where joyful thoughts begin to spin.

Potted plants wear funny hats,
Giggling gnomes and sneaky cats.
A leaf that tickles, brings a chuckle,
In this jungle, we all snuggle.

Bright colors leap from shelf to shelf,
As if they're playing with themselves.
A palm tree sways to tunes of cheer,
Whispering jokes for all to hear.

In this garden where joy expands,
I sit with sunshine in my hands.
The canopy, my playful muse,
Sows seeds of laughter, pure amuse.

Warm Breezes in a Glass

A sip of sun in every gulp,
Straws that wiggle, dance and pulp.
Liquid limes and fruity highs,
Together, let's invent the skies.

Coconuts roll in laughter,
As mimosas burst with cheer hereafter.
Shaking ice and laughing too,
With every clink, we start anew.

The blender hums a joyful tune,
While the clock dials back to noon.
Cheers to the peppy little sips,
Time for jokes and friendly quips.

In this glass, the breezes swirl,
Mixed together with a twirl.
So raise your cup and let's make haste,
To be silly with zesty waste!

Nightfall in the Greenhouse

As darkness tiptoes, plants take flight,
Whispering secrets in the night.
The moon's a jester, shining bright,
With sleepy giggles, oh, what a sight!

Mossy beds with crickets sing,
Antics of the night take wing.
Dewdrops play hide-and-seek,
While shadows chuckle, oh so chic.

Glowing bugs flash a cheeky grin,
Inviting mischief, come on in!
Tropical dreams fill the air,
With laughter hiding everywhere.

In this greenhouse, joy takes root,
As flowers don their party suits.
Nightfall wears a playful face,
Creating mischief at a frolic pace.

Tropical Reverie

In daydreams where the sunshine's bold,
Parrots shout jokes, stories told.
A hammock sways with gentle glee,
While thoughts drift like a yellow bee.

Coconut hats on wise old trees,
Sway and chuckle in the breeze.
The sunbeams tickle, making me laugh,
What a whimsical photograph!

In this vision, absurdity reigns,
Watermelon smiles, monkey trains.
The ocean waves clap their hands,
Cheering on silly, playful bands.

Let's dance among the flowing bliss,
Where dreams bloom, who could resist?
A vibrant world, spun like a tale,
In this reverie, we shall prevail!

A Tropical Reverie

In my cozy space, trees do sway,
Palm fronds dance, like they want to play.
Sipping juice from a plastic cup,
Imagining waves, should I surf or sup?

A parrot squawks, 'Where's my drink?'
While the sun fades, I start to think.
My cat's a tiger, prowls my bed,
Laughing as I lay my weary head.

Cactus jokes in a sandy plot,
One-liners bloom, oh what a lot!
Sipping coconuts that aren't even round,
In this jungle, fun's always found.

Me and my plants, a lively crew,
Laughing at clouds that yell, "We're blue!"
With slippers like flip-flops, we groove,
In this paradise, we all can move.

Green Dreams Amidst Four Walls

Vines creep close, they're planning to hug,
Worn-out rugs bloom like a bug.
A fern whispers secrets, oh so sly,
While I grumble, 'Why'd you take my pie?'

The potted palms are fierce and bold,
Blame them when the room gets cold.
They huddle close, in leafy talks,
Swapping tales with the purple socks.

Laughter rolls like waves on sand,
Who's watering whom? Not what I planned!
A world of green, all around me spins,
Playing hide and seek with my twin chins.

At sunset, I wear a plant crown proud,
Dancing with chlorophyll, laughter loud.
Living in this lush-made zone,
A funny jungle, all my own.

The Warmth of Island Light

My window glares like a conch shell,
Pretending to be an island hotel.
Laughter rides the humid breeze,
While I search my snack stash with ease.

The sunshine tickles my flimsy chair,
I knock over a plant, but I don't care.
"Grow up!" I yell at the tangled vines,
They giggle back, 'We'll be fine!'

A dance party erupts with my gear,
Socks in sandals, nothing to fear.
The carpet waves like an ocean bed,
While I do the hula, feeling well-fed.

Waves slide in with an audio track,
My blender hums, it's got my back.
In my sunny room, fun's taken flight,
Island vibes are always in sight.

Secrets of a Leafy Sanctuary

In my fortress of greenery, secrets grow,
Monstera leaves whisper, 'Take it slow.'
An iguana sunbathes on my desk,
But it's really just my pillow, quite grotesque.

Buzzy bees buzz from a jar of honey,
Dancing on air, aren't they funny?
A lizard falls off its leafy throne,
Lands in my popcorn bowl with a groan.

Down the fern path, I hear a tune,
From a radio stuck to a paper moon.
The floor is a beach, I kick my feet,
Sandy toes are quite the treat!

In this haven where laughter blooms,
I trip over shoes and dodge the brooms.
Life's a party, and it's just begun,
In my leafy hideout, we're having fun!

Sounds of Serendipity

In the corner, a parrot squawks,
Telling tales of silly walks.
A tropical breeze, it flaps its wings,
While I dance like I'm in a ring.

Coconuts roll across the floor,
Bouncing off the open door.
I declare a floor is my stage,
And with each step, I disengage.

Basil plants jump with glee,
Greenery joins my folly spree.
The laughter of vines fills the air,
As I juggle with mangoes in flare.

In this room, I'm much too spry,
Not a soul to hear me cry!
The sounds of joy, a wild serenade,
In my garden of strange charades.

Illuminated Botanicals

Lights hang like fruit from the sky,
Each plant tells jokes, oh my, oh my!
Succulents joke about their thirst,
I laugh so hard, I'm bound to burst.

Cacti tease with their prickly air,
Saying, "Touch me if you dare!"
Bananas swing like they're so cool,
I slip and slide—what a fool!

Lemon leaves giggle, chatting bright,
They pull stunts in the pale moonlight.
With every flicker and playful sway,
Their laughter makes the night's ballet.

In this room, nonsense does thrive,
With vibrant greens, I'm quite alive!
Botanicals blend in a riotous tune,
Making me chuckle beneath the moon.

Sunset Shadows on the Wall

As the sun dips low, shadows dance,
On the wall, they prance and prance.
A lizard dons a cape of light,
Declaring himself the king tonight.

Each flicker a secret, oh what fun!
Silly gnomes join the race to run.
With colors splashed like a painter's dream,
Who knew a wall could have such gleam?

Vines wrap around like they're in a play,
Twisting and twirling, hip-hip hooray!
A chorus of hues, nothing to fear,
They all frolic as shadows cheer.

Laughter echoes as dusk begins,
In this room, the joy never thins.
Sunset whispers, "Just let it flow,"
Creating moments we all will know.

Whispering Palms in Paradise

Palms sway gently, a secret shush,
"Dance with us!" they say in a hush.
Their fronds tickle like a soft hand,
As I shuffle across this sandy land.

They gossip tales of the winds they meet,
Twisting and turning, oh so sweet.
My ceiling fans join the wild parade,
Turning fast, they all cascade.

With every rustling, giggles ignite,
Casting a spell on this silly night.
I hear their voices, playful and wise,
Making fun of the clouds in disguise.

If life's a beach, I'm lost in mirth,
Each palm a jester of infinite worth.
In good cheer, they whisper away,
Creating nonsense in the light of day.

Driftwood and Daydreams

A palm tree waves, a cheeky grin,
Its coconut buddy lets the fun begin.
Tangled strings of fairy lights,
Dance with shadows on summer nights.

Sipping from a plastic cup,
As ocean thoughts spill out and up.
Seashells chatter in the breeze,
While I lounge with a snack of cheese.

A dolphin leaps, but wait—it's foam,
Splashing laughter, it feels like home.
The sun just winked; oh, could it be?
That it's just playing tricks on me?

Driftwood tales float on my wall,
A beachy vibe for one and all.
I trip on dreams, they trip on me,
This room's a trip - oh, look at thee!

Serene Vignettes of Paradise

A lizard sunbathes on the sill,
While I engage in a quiet thrill.
Cactus dance with graceful flair,
Each prickly joke fills up the air.

Tropical blooms in a vase run wild,
Petals giggle like a playful child.
Sunlight filters with a warm embrace,
As I pretend it's a seaside place.

Mango dreams drip down my chin,
As I laugh at all that's 'been.
A cheeky parrot mimics me,
I raise the stakes with coconut tea.

The ceiling fans start to hum a tune,
As if to say it's time to swoon.
Here in my nook, all feels just right,
Living with laughs from day till night.

Sol with a Splash of Shade

Sunshine bursts through the window's frame,
Each beam of light seems to play a game.
Shadows giggle as they skitter,
In this room, my heart's a glitter.

Infusions swirl in my desk-bound drink,
A little umbrella makes me think.
Of tuk-tuk rides and joyful mobs,
As laughter dances with the blobs.

Hammocks swing in my mind's broad sway,
It's Friday—every day, they say!
Flip-flops grazing tiles, what a sound,
Could this funny corner be found?

On paper beaches, I'll sketch and draw,
With a smile as wide as a yaw.
This space is filled with sunny cheer,
Who knew such fun could live right here?

Sanctuary of Silhouettes

Candles flicker, casting shapes,
In a world where the funny drapes.
A toucan's peak, an 'ahem' so sly,
Winks and flutters as it flits by.

My shadows sway with a tropical beat,
As fruits fall over in the seat.
Comedy blooms, all in good jest,
In a bumpy hammock, I'll find some rest.

Soft whispers from a colorful fish,
Requesting my most shocking wish.
That my nap would last till the moon,
Comedic rhymes in a playful tune.

Pineapple hats on a spooky ghost,
Laughing with me, they love the coast.
A silly sanctuary, full of cheer,
In my wildest dreams, all's crystal clear.

Pulse of the Rain

Raindrops dance on the ceiling,
A symphony of tickles and squeals.
Puddles form on the tiled floor,
Ducks in my mind, making deals.

The curtain sways like a dancer,
In rhythm with nature's sweet tune.
A drip here, a splash there,
I giggle at each little swoon.

My socks are all drenched and soggy,
Yet laughter makes them feel light.
Who needs a raincoat or umbrella?
This indoor storm is pure delight!

Sometimes thunder rumbles loudly,
But I just roll on the bed.
Making waves with my tossed-out shoes,
A sailor lost in my head!

Sun-kissed Refuge

Sunbeams sneak through the curtains,
Spilling gold on the crunchy floor.
I've invited the light inside,
Now it's a beach, not a bore!

With my chair turned into a throne,
I sip Gatorade like fine brew.
The sun's my artist, painting joy,
While I play pirates—ahoy, crew!

Cushions like clouds under my feet,
A dive into cozy, warm foam.
Tanned like a lizard in the sun,
This living room, my sandy home!

I wear sunglasses like a star,
Dancing with an imaginary band.
Coconut-scented air surrounds,
I'll call this paradise, so grand!

Mysteries of Monsoon

Mystic clouds play hide-and-seek,
While I float in a bubble bath.
My rubber duck, a captain bold,
Guides me through the stormy path.

Raindrops leak through the window,
They tickle my planner, embarking,
Plans for tea parties and laughter,
While outside, the lightning's sparking!

I peek at the skies, a detective,
With an umbrella, my trusty sidekick.
Each boisterous splash a giggle,
As I dodge the monsoon's quick flick!

Rivers run wild down my street,
But I'm in my own wonderland.
With every storm that breaks the day,
I create my own joy so grand!

Fresh Air Fantasia

The window's wide, the breeze comes in,
Tickling my cheeks, what a tease!
I dance like a noodle, unhinged,
A whirling dervish with ease.

Fragrant spices float like dreams,
Mixing with air and my snacks.
Elvis lives in my blender,
As I spin to the rhythm, no lacks!

Limes and ginger sing their sweet tunes,
Chaotic flavors fill the air.
I'm a chef in my sitcom show,
With outfits made for comedy flair!

Every crinkle brings scenes alive,
I cook up worlds with a grin.
In this crazy, vibrant escape,
Even the plants join in on the spin!

Indoor Rainforest Symphony

In my living room, a vine does swing,
Monkeys in pajamas, oh what a thing!
The couch is a rock, the coffee a brook,
A symphony plays, from my book, a great nook.

A parrot's request for chips is quite bold,
He squawks for salsa, thinks he's so old!
Leaves rustle gently; who's hoofing around?
A raccoon with snacks, I cannot be found.

Giant ferns dance, as a breeze swells near,
Tickling my toes, as I munch on my cheer.
A waterfall trickles from the fridge's door,
In this wild habitat, I couldn't ask for more!

The sunbeams peek in, where the shadows delight,
Creating a party that lasts through the night.
With laughter and chaos, a jungle so grand,
Who knew my living room was a wild wonderland?

Silken Breeze of Faraway Lands

A gust of soft wind in my tiny space,
Brings whispers of islands and a sunlit embrace.
I sip coconut milk, in a palm leaf so wide,
Pretend I'm on beaches, with sand on my side.

A safari of snacks, where colors collide,
With gummy bears taking their sweet little stride.
Lemon drops thunder, on this fruity parade,
While licorice lizards hold sweet cavalcade.

Hammocks of towels sway gently in air,
Shrunken explorer sits, without a care.
He pulls out a map made of marshmallows bright,
Guiding us all on an edible flight.

Tropical rhythms, a dance that we do,
In my living space, creativity blooms.
With giggles and sunshine that makes my heart sing,
Who doesn't love a cheerful indoor fling?

Vibrant Visions in Soft Light

In the glow of twilight, the colors ignite,
A kaleidoscope world, oh what a sight!
Pillows like clouds, and blankets are streams,
I float on my sofa, lost in my dreams.

A butterfly darts past, in polka-dot flair,
Spreading bright giggles, floating in air.
Socks turned to birds, swooping to play,
As I summon a rainstorm in whimsical spray.

The curtains sway gently, as if in a dance,
Inviting old slippers to join in the chance.
Sunflowers giggle, on each painted wall,
While laughter ripples like a soft waterfall.

With whimsical figures igniting my night,
Imagination blooms in fanciful light.
Creating a haven where giggles can soar,
This colorful chaos, I simply adore!

The Jungle Beneath My Bed

Under my bed, where the wild things creep,
A land of plush creatures who never sleep.
Cushions become mountains, with valleys in view,
Where dreams can parade, and adventures accrue.

A stuffed bear, my captain, leads the way strong,
Through jungles of socks, where silence feels wrong.
The dust bunnies giggle, they throw me a glance,
It's a wild expedition, a rare happenstance.

Treasure maps sketched in crayon delight,
In quest of the snacks hidden quite out of sight.
Pirate ships made of Lego sail past my toes,
As giggles explode, oh, the fun never slows!

With pillows for boats, we navigate seas,
Each splash brings a giggle, each wave brings the breeze.
In this jungle below, on my floor, I declare,
There's magic in chaos and joy in the flares!

Lush Dreams Whispers

In a jungle of pillows, I sleep tight,
Pajamas made of parrots, what a sight!
Banana peels serve as my comfy sheets,
Waking up to monkeys and tropical beats.

Coconuts whisper sweet secrets at night,
While flamingos dance, oh what a delight!
A hammock made of dreams, I swing and sway,
Where laundry's a luau every single day.

Lizards in sunglasses, talk about style,
They laugh at my hair, but just for a while.
Sunshine spills laughter all over the floor,
I sip my juice, and my troubles are no more.

Sunlight Serenade

Sunbeams bounce off my cereal bowl,
Offering breakfast with a tropical soul.
Pineapple slices, a funny affair,
That dance on my toast, beyond the compare.

Inkwell of mango, I spill with a grin,
As a parrot claims rights to the jam with a spin.
Squirrels in grass skirts join in for the fun,
While I juggle fruits under the bright, warm sun.

Each afternoon, I try not to slack,
With dance moves that surely can cause a heart attack.
Guess the coconuts took an interest too,
In learning my moves, oh what a hullabaloo!

Swaying Palms at Dawn

Palm fronds wave as if saying, 'Hello!'
While I bumble around in my grass skirt show.
A parrot critiques my dance moves with glee,
I shrug, it's not easy, just let me be free!

The morning sun tickles my sleepy old toes,
As I trip on a flip-flop, oh, how it goes!
Fish in a bowl laugh, I swear it is true,
Judging my outfits; what could I do?

Melons provide shade when I feel like a snack,
Failing at yoga, I might fall back.
A lion-shaped rug says, 'Try it again!'
As I wiggle and giggle and finally ascend.

Bottled Oasis

This bottle's a boat stuck on my desk,
With seashells and fish, oh what a mess!
Sipping on soda that sparkles like night,
As seagulls complain that I'm not quite polite.

Turtles in ties plan a grand parade,
While I pop popcorn to celebrate the trade.
My chair is a raft on a river of dreams,
Riding the currents of silly extremes.

Bubble wrap islands, I hop like a kid,
Till a crab in a tuxedo darts from his lid.
Where laughter resounds, it's a joy ride, indeed,
In this bottled-up world, happiness is freed.

A Haven of Warmth and Whimsy

Sunshine sprawls across my floor,
A lizard naps by the door.
Cacti wear such silly hats,
My pet parrot chats with the cats.

Palm trees sway, they seem to dance,
In their embrace, I take a chance.
A hammock stretched, I lie and swing,
While a rubber ducky wears a bling.

My blender hums a tropical tune,
As I sip from a giant spoon.
Breezy fans that spin so slow,
Shake maracas with a flow.

Each plant's a character, oh so bright,
They gossip softly in the night.
With laughter's echo in the air,
This playful space shows love and care.

Leafy Retreat from the World

Vines are chatting on the wall,
One looks shy, the other tall.
Ferns gossip like old friends,
Spilling secrets as time bends.

A sloth hangs from a fake high vine,
Waves his hand, 'Hey, you're fine!'
Bamboo spritzing water's fun,
A splash of mist from morning sun.

Cushions shaped like fruits abound,
Fruits mock the couch as it astounds.
I giggle at the sight so lush,
When the blender starts to rush.

The clock ticks slowly, oh so sly,
While fancy bugs give wings a try.
A laughter-filled retreat unspun,
Here the world outside seems done.

Serene Shores Within Walls

Seashells scattered on my floor,
Starfish beckon, 'Want some more?'
They whisper tales of ocean's call,
In my hideaway, I stand tall.

An aquarium's colors flash and swirl,
Goldfish twirl like a ballerina's whurl.
The tide's a friend that sings to me,
With waves of jest, I'm wild and free.

Coconut-scented candles burn,
Dancing flames provide the churn.
With every puff that fills the air,
I find my bliss with nary a care.

A beach ball rolls, it tries to hide,
Filling up the empty side.
In this serene and silly space,
Joy's the current, laughter's race.

Garlands of Color and Comfort

Tangled lights hang everywhere,
A rainbow shines in my hair.
Lumpy pillows, bright and bold,
Whisper stories yet untold.

Paper lanterns swing on high,
As I dance and give a sigh.
A carpet sprawls like grass outdoors,
Transforming rooms to outdoor shores.

Chalk drawings on the floor,
Scribbles like there's nothing more.
My teddy bear's a hula king,
As ukuleles start to sing.

In every corner, laughs take flight,
Even shadows join delight.
This space of chaos, sweet and wild,
Is where life's fun is always piled.

Vine-Clothed Imaginations

In the corner, a plant starts to twirl,
With thoughts of a jungle, it gives a whirl.
I swear it whispers secrets at night,
Of vines and limes and pure delight.

Pillows are mountains, soft as a cloud,
Each time I jump, I'm cheering loud.
My cat's a tiger, fierce and spry,
To nap in wonder, oh my, oh my!

The pictures on the wall come to life,
Dancing together, avoiding their strife.
A monkey escapes, swinging near,
I need a quick snack, or I'll shed a tear.

Moody frogs croak in chorus so sweet,
They throw a party, full of grace and heat.
With laughter erupting from every leaf,
Who needs an island for silly relief?

The Echo of Ocean Waves

Inside my room, there's a beach ball,
Swaying gently, ready to sprawl.
It tells of tides, of moonlit nights,
And the thrill of fish in daring flights.

A shell from my last trip sits on the sill,
It sighs and murmurs, gives me a thrill.
Sandy footprints dance on my floor,
My floor mat is now a tropical shore.

A seagull's squawk, a laugh or two,
My pet fish giggles, he knows it's true.
I wear shades indoors, just for the fun,
Pretending I'm basking under the sun.

The waves of laughter, they crash and play,
As I drift to dream like the end of the day.
What a fabulous place to take a snooze,
With ocean whispers and funny news!

Paradise in a Windowframe

Outside the glass, the world may seem,
But in my space, it's a lively dream.
Sunlight paints pictures of bliss,
Where I chase coconuts, say 'Oh, what a miss!'

Birds serenade in hilarious tones,
While I build castles with mismatched stones.
A sun hat sitting on my head,
My book's a treasure map, oh what fun it led!

The breeze teases curtains, a silly fan,
Like a playful dancer, doing its plan.
Cacti in pots do a wiggle and sway,
They laugh at my dance, in a prickly way.

With fruits in the fridge that giggle and grin,
I craft smoothies thick, let sweet chaos begin.
There's joy in my nook that's perfectly bright,
In every corner, there's pure delight!

Aroma of Citrus Dreams

The smell of oranges fills my space,
As I pull up chairs, it's a sweet embrace.
Lemonade rivers flow in my mind,
Will this Sunday ever unwind?

A grapefruit rolls; it's a round little chap,
Beneath a fruit tree, I plan my nap.
Limes do a tango, zesting the air,
As giggles erupt from everywhere.

Under bright lights, I dance with glee,
Squirrels and fruit flies, they join my spree.
I wear a crown of peels on my head,
In this citrus kingdom, I shall be fed!

From this colorful chaos, joy proceeds,
Sweet scents and laughter, my heart proceeds.
What a festival of flavors, ripe and wild,
Every hour here feels wonderfully styled!

Hidden Rainforest

In my clutter, a jungle grows,
Plants hang out, in lovely rows.
A parrot squawks, does it know?
Or just judging from its show?

I water them like I'm a pro,
Yet they thrive, in spite of woe.
Vines slither down in disco flair,
Beneath this roof, we breathe fresh air!

My cat prowls like a fierce lion,
But she's more like a sleepy pylon.
She waits for a toy made of string,
Then leaps, as if a jungle king!

Life here's wild, with laughter loud,
A wild side hidden, under a cloud.
So come join this indoor spree,
In this rainforest made just for me!

Crickets and Candlelight

The crickets chirp a funny tune,
In the glow of a candle's moon.
They dance around on my night stand,
Like tiny stars on a wild land.

The wax drips like a silly stream,
Creating shadows that gleam and beam.
I swear they're playing a joke on me,
Why is my room a concert spree?

I hum along, it's quite absurd,
Twirling with a dim-lit bird.
A firefly thinks it's a disco ball,
And I'm here for it all, after all!

I sip from a teacup of dreams,
Where nothing is what it seems.
These evenings, filled with chirpy cheer,
Are the best moments I hold dear!

The Color of Calm

In my space of vibrant hues,
Where every corner tells some news.
A bright blue chair, a pinkish rug,
Each color gives my heart a hug.

Green pillows waving with a breeze,
A sanctuary that aims to please.
I recline, listening to the sound,
Of calmness laughter all around.

Stripes and polka dots take the stage,
I'm in love with this color cage.
Thoughts of rainbows twist and twine,
In this cheerful little shrine!

The walls giggle, the floors hum back,
In this kaleidoscopic track.
It's a cozy burst of sunny fun,
Where the day is brighter, never done!

Woven Sunbeams

Sunbeams thread through window panes,
Like golden lines in wacky chains.
I dance between their radiant lies,
While dust motes float in giggly sighs.

A hammock swings with a silly twist,
"Forget your worries, come take a risk!"
I bounce like a butterfly at play,
My room's a beach, come seize the day!

Laughter echoes 'neath a quilt,
Where dreams are sown and joy is built.
Each woven thread, a giggle spun,
In the rays of warmth, we have our fun.

So I'll soak in this tangled light,
Turning mundane into delight.
With every ray that colors my space,
I find my heart in a sunny embrace!

The Garden Between Thoughts

In my mind's garden, weeds do bloom,
They dance in hats, they hope for room.
A gnome juggles thoughts with silly flair,
While ladybugs gossip without a care.

Petunias giggle, that's quite the sight,
They chat about daisies shining bright.
A trampoline swings from the tulip's head,
Where fairies bounce—oh, aren't they fed?

Caterpillars don tuxedos to prance,
While worms hold hands and spin a dance.
A sunbeam slides down a broccoli tree,
Saying, "Join this party, won't you see?"

So here I linger, thoughts in bloom,
In my mind's garden, there's always room.
With laughter growing where whispers roam,
In this colorful chaos, I feel at home.

Soft Glow of Island Hues

Under a palm made of cotton candy,
I sip my drink, oh-so-sandy.
A parrot wears shades, looking so cool,
While crabs try surfing, but never rule.

The sun is a wink, teasing the sea,
As pineapple hats dance wild and free.
Turtles with surfboards challenged the tide,
But all they did was tumble and slide.

Coconuts giggle as seagulls rehearse,
For a musical number, though it's quite terse.
With beach balls bouncing on waves that chuckle,
And seashells clap, oh what a snuggle!

So here I bask in hues so bright,
With laughter and joy, my daily delight.
A paradise not found on a map,
Just a silly dream where I happily nap.

Sweet Serenity Wrapped in Green

A hammock swings between two trees,
While squirrels tell tales of summer breeze.
The leaves are whispers, secrets they keep,
As ants march by in a marching leap.

Sunflowers wear hats that stretch to the sky,
While butterflies zip with a curious fly.
Mossy carpets invite me to sprawl,
In this green wonderland, I have it all.

A frog plays chess with a curious snail,
Wagering stories of epic scale.
Daisies giggle as bumblebees buzz,
With nature, it seems, I'm always in a fuzz.

So here I lounge, wrapped up in green,
In a world where nothing is quite as it seems.
With amusing antics that tickle my mind,
In sweet serenity, my joy I find.

A Symphony of Nature's Palette

In the orchestra of trees, the branches sway,
While flowers hum tunes that brighten the day.
Bees play the trumpet with buzzing delight,
As crickets join in, singing all night.

A rainbow's a painter, splatting its hues,
As clouds throw shadows, adding their cues.
Each leaf's a note in this vibrant score,
Where laughter and joy echo evermore.

The brook is a clarinet, bubbly and bold,
With frogs as the backup, a sight to behold.
A snail takes a solo, slow but so grand,
In this symphony where fun is all planned.

So, let us dance to this playful tune,
With nature's palette beneath the moon.
In this concert of life, I twirl and spin,
With a chuckle and grin, let the laughter begin!

Embrace of Exotic Flora

In the corner, a plant waves,
It's dancing to the music I play.
With big leaves, it's quite the show,
I wonder if it knows how to sway.

A cactus joins in, prickly with flair,
Wearing sunglasses, it's quite bold.
It says, 'Chill out, let down your hair,'
While sipping on sunshine, or so I'm told.

A fern whispers, secrets of green,
It tickles my nose, what a tease!
With every breath, a new sheen,
Oh nature, you come with such ease.

In this jungle of whims, I lounge,
Puns sprout like vines, everywhere.
My house is wild, it's quite a proud binge,
The plants, they laugh – oh, how they dare!

Quietude of the Tropics

In my cozy cocoon, I hide,
A llama plushie is my best friend.
It guards my dreams, standing with pride,
While a parrot squawks, 'Hey, don't pretend!'

The walls are painted in bright hues,
Like a sunset that doesn't fade.
They shout, 'Let's play and have some blues!'
I guess it's the vibe I've made.

A hammock swings with lazy grace,
Where I ponder mysteries of life.
It asks for fruit, a sweet embrace,
As I giggle, avoiding all strife.

In this retreat, with a wink and a grin,
Nature's laughter fills the air.
I'm just a kid lost in my skin,
Forget the world, who really cares?

Fragrant Footprints

With tropical scents held in the breeze,
I step outside where the laughter blooms.
Bamboo softens all of my knees,
While butterflies tease in bright costumes.

The mango tree calls, 'Come take a break!',
Its fruits are secrets just waiting to spill.
I grab one and laugh, 'What a sweet mistake!'
As juice drips down, it's a sticky thrill.

A coconut bounces, says, "Try my hat!"
Balancing it is a comical feat.
I twirl like a dancer, not sure where I'm at,
Guess I'll blend in like a fruit salad treat!

Life's a parade in this quirky plot,
With joyous blooms that won't hold still.
Each step echoing what fun I've got,
In fragrant footprints, my heart will thrill!

Haven of Hibiscus

Nestled among petals, I rest with glee,
The hibiscus mocks with a bright, red pout.
'You think you're funny? Come laugh with me!'
We giggle at shadows, that's what it's about.

My rubber plant's a therapist, wise and tall,
'Tell me your secrets,' it says with a grin.
As I spill all, it pretends not to call,
Laughing as leaves dance with gentle spin.

A gecko watches from its leafy throne,
Winking like it knows all my schemes.
It infiltrates plans I thought were my own,
While plotting escapes in colorful dreams.

In this charming void of wild, carefree play,
The world beyond fades to a hum.
Let's frolic with plants, what more can I say?
In a haven of hues, there's never a glum!

The Essence of Sun-Kissed Moments

Beneath the shades where piña coladas flow,
My couch transforms to a beach, don't you know?
With flip-flops dancing on the living room floor,
I sip on sunshine, who could ask for more?

Cushions like coconuts, fluffy and round,
They're palm trees swaying, no worries abound.
I chase the rays, with a pillow for shade,
Laughing at life's beachy masquerade.

The TV plays waves while I kick back and grin,
I'm the captain here, let the adventures begin!
In my sea of snacks, I sail on a chair,
Navigating dreams, with a tropical flair.

So bring on the sun, let the mischief ignite,
In this garden of giggles, it feels just right.
With each sun-kissed moment, I giggle and say,
Who knew paradise was a room far away?

Exotic Whispers in the Air

In a jungle of socks, where wild patterns play,
My laundry has turned into a wild cabaret!
With each gentle breeze, I hear the trees hum,
It's a party of fruits – oh, here they come!

Bananas in hats swinging left and right,
Mangoes toss confetti, what a curious sight!
Papayas do the limbo, oh my, oh dear,
As I dance with a cactus, sipping cold beer.

The walls are alive, they chuckle and cheer,
With walls of bright colors, I have nothing to fear.
Lizards at my feet, they wiggle and wink,
In this room of delight, we're all on the brink.

So grab your decor, let's blend and collide,
With exotic whispers, let our laughter ride.
In a realm where normal becomes quite absurd,
I find joy in the silly, and let go of my word.

Soft Bamboo in the Breeze

In the corner, a plant waves, oh so polite,
Bamboo's got moves that are light and bright.
It giggles with shadows, as sunlight has fun,
While I'm munching on chips, feeling like a bun.

The floor creaks like a boat in a gentle sea,
As I navigate snacks, laughing blissfully.
With cushions of green, my chair starts to sway,
Like a bamboo forest, lively in play.

Plucking the strings of my ukulele delight,
I serenade snacks in the soft evening light.
The neighbors might wonder what party goes on,
But this tune of my heart is a wild tropical song.

So here's to the whispers of bamboo and cheer,
In this wild little world, I hold dear,
Embracing the silliness, dancing with glee,
In my funny jungle, forever carefree.

Comfort of Mango-Scented Dreams

At midnight, the mangoes start to conspire,
In a fruity rebellion, they're fueled by desire.
With pillows as clouds, I float through delight,
In a dream full of laughter, all through the night.

They giggle and tumble, running amok,
As I clutch my smoothie, feeling quite stuck.
The mango brigade waves, spiky and sweet,
In this cozy confusion, I dance on my feet.

The ceiling becomes a tropical sky,
With twinkling stars made of citrus to fly.
As I snuggle with laughter, my dreams come alive,
In this fruity fiesta, we happily thrive.

So let's dive into dreams of mango delight,
Where whimsy is king, and all feels so right.
In this room of comfort, I giggle and scheme,
Wrapped in the essence of soft, sweet dreams.

www.ingramcontent.com/pod-product-compliance
Lightning Source LLC
Chambersburg PA
CBHW070327120526
44590CB00017B/2825